Food and Festivals

WEST AFRICA

Alison Brownlie

RAINTREE
STECK-VAUGHN
PUBLISHERS
A Steck-Vaughn Company

Austin, Texas

Other titles:

The Caribbean ● China ● India
Mexico ● West Africa

Cover photograph: Carrying mangoes at a market in Burkina Faso

Title page: Women at a festival in Benin, Nigeria, playing musical instruments

Contents page: Frying yams in Nigeria

Published by Raintree Steck-Vaughn Publishers, an imprint of Steck-Vaughn Company

Printed in Italy. Bound in the United States.
1 2 3 4 5 6 7 8 9 0 03 02 01 00 99

Library of Congress Cataloging-in-Publication Data
Brownlie, Alison.
West Africa / Alison Brownlie.
    p.   cm.—(Food and festivals)
    Includes bibliographical references and index.
    Summary: Describes the West African culture of food, including the kinds of food grown and eaten, and various feast days like Ramadan, Easter, naming ceremonies, and yam festivals.
    ISBN 0-8172-5552-4
    1. Cookery, West African—Juvenile literature.
    2. Food habits—Africa, West—Juvenile literature.
    3. Festivals—Africa, West—Juvenile literature.
    4. Africa, West—Social life and customs—Juvenile literature.
    [1. Cookery, West African. 2. Food habits—Africa, West. 3. Festivals—Africa, West. 4. Africa, West—Social life and customs.]
    I. Title. II. Series.
TX725.W47B76 1999
394.1'0966—dc21   98-25102

CONTENTS

West Africa and Its Food   4

Food and Farming   6

Ramadan and Id-ul-Fitr   12

Easter in Sierra Leone   18

Naming Ceremonies   22

Yam Festivals   26

Glossary   30

Books to Read   31

Index   32

West Africa and Its Food

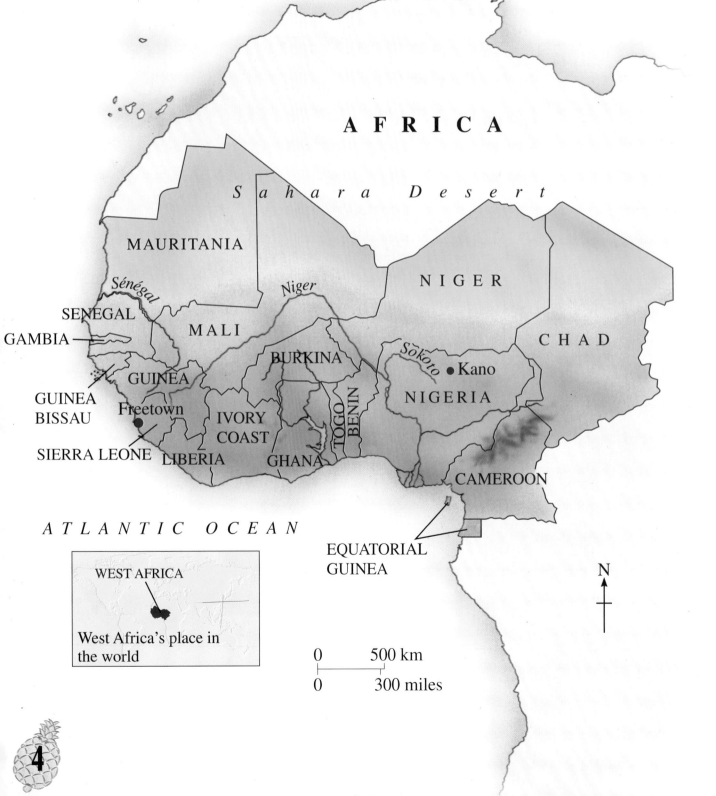

AFRICA

Sahara Desert

MAURITANIA

Sénégal

Niger

SENEGAL

GAMBIA

MALI

NIGER

CHAD

BURKINA

Sokoto

GUINEA

• Kano

GUINEA
BISSAU

Freetown

IVORY
COAST

TOGO

BENIN

NIGERIA

SIERRA LEONE

LIBERIA

GHANA

CAMEROON

ATLANTIC OCEAN

EQUATORIAL
GUINEA

N

WEST AFRICA

West Africa's place in
the world

0   500 km

0   300 miles

Millet and corn

Millet and corn are both grain crops, like rice. Grain crops are among the main foods for most people in West Africa.

Fish

Fish and seafood are an important source of protein for people who live near the coast or a river.

Yams and cassava

Yams and cassava are the other main foods in West Africa. They are both root vegetables, which means that they grow underground.

Peanuts

Peanuts, which are also called groundnuts, are really a type of bean. They are a main food crop in the dry north.

Cattle, sheep, and goats

These animals are kept mainly for their milk. Farmers in the north move their cattle around in herds and sell them for meat.

Fruit

Fruits such as mangoes, coconuts, pineapples, and bananas grow on plantations, as well as in the wild.

Food and Farming

West Africa is a vast region in Africa, made up of seventeen different countries. More than 182 million people live there. West Africa has many landscapes. In the south, along the coast, it is hot and rainy all year round. There, thick rain forests cover the land. Farther north, where the climate is drier, there are grassy plains and deserts. The climate of West Africa affects the type of food that is grown.

In dry Mauritania, two nomads milk a camel.

Millet, corn, and rice

Millet and corn are two of the main foods in West Africa. Millet grows easily in the drier, northern areas of West Africa. Corn needs more water than millet, so it grows farther south. Both corn and millet are usually pounded into flour and used to make porridge and cakes. Rice grows only in the wetter south of the region or near rivers.

These women in Mali are winnowing millet.

Yams, cassava, and peanuts

The most important vegetables in West Africa are yams, cassava, and peanuts. Yams and cassava are both root crops, like potatoes. Their thick, white roots are either peeled or grated before they are cooked. Sometimes yams are pounded into *fufu*, which is like mashed potatoes. Cassava must be cooked carefully, because it is poisonous if it is eaten raw.

Peanuts grow easily in the dry north. They were brought there from South America by the Portuguese, more than 500 years ago.

This boy is grating cassava in Ghana.

HARVEST FESTIVALS

All over West Africa, festivals are held to celebrate the harvest of the main food that grows in the area. Guinea and Sierra Leone have a rice festival at harvesttime. In villages near the sea, people hold festivals to celebrate the fish catch. The most famous harvest festival in West Africa is the yam festival, which is held in most African countries.

8

◀ This girl is tending her family's goats, in Ghana.

Chickens, goats, and cattle

Most West African farmers have a few goats or chickens. Goats and cattle are kept mainly for their milk. Chickens are kept for their meat and for their eggs.

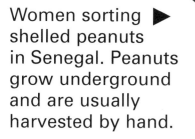

Women sorting ▶ shelled peanuts in Senegal. Peanuts grow underground and are usually harvested by hand.

FISH FESTIVALS

The lively fish festival of Argungu takes place on the Sokoto River in Nigeria every year. The men have a competition to see who can catch the biggest fish. They use calabashes and nets, which are traditional fishing tools. The winners receive prizes, usually money.

The Hausa people of Nigeria take part in the Argungu fish festival.

Fish

Fish and seafood are important foods for people who live near the coast or near rivers such as the Senegal or the Niger. These foods contain protein, which helps the body to grow. Fish is often smoked over a fire to preserve it. Since fish is quite expensive, many people eat it only on special occasions.

People and religions

People in West Africa come from many different backgrounds, with their own languages, religions, and traditions. That is because people have come to West Africa from other countries over hundreds of years, bringing their religions and customs with them. These have influenced the food and festivals in West Africa today.

Many people in West Africa, especially in the north and west, are Muslims. They follow the religion of Islam. In Senegal and Gambia, 90 percent of the people are Muslims.

These guards, in northern Nigeria, are Muslims. They work for the emir, who is the local ruler.

Ramadan and Id-ul-Fitr

The month of Ramadan is the most holy occasion in the Muslim religion. During this month, every year, most Muslims do not eat or drink between sunrise and sunset. They fast to obey the Muslim holy book, called the Koran, and to remind themselves that all food comes from Allah.

Praying to Allah at the end of Ramadan, in Cameroon

Fasting during the day for a whole month is quite difficult. Children under the age of about twelve, pregnant women, and the sick and elderly do not have to take part in the fast.

Id-ul-Fitr

In the Muslim calendar, the months do not begin and end on fixed dates. Instead, a new month begins when the new moon appears. When the Imam (the religious leader of a town or area) sees the new moon at the end of Ramadan, it is time for the festival of Id-ul-Fitr to begin.

The festival begins with the beating of a drum. People dress in their best clothes and go to the mosque to say their prayers. They pray on special prayer mats or on colorful rugs.

FORBIDDEN FOOD

In the Muslim holy book, the Koran, certain foods are forbidden. Muslims are not allowed to eat pork.

Men in Nigeria beating different types of drums

13

This street procession is held at the start of Id-ul-Fitr, in the city of Kano, Nigeria.

Processions and presents

There are processions through many villages at Id-ul-Fitr. In northern Nigeria there is a huge, colorful parade called a *sallah*. People crowd through the streets to the emir's palace. There, men on horseback charge forward to salute the emir.

An important part of Id-ul-Fitr is giving to the poor. People also visit friends and give presents of candy. Eating, drinking, and dancing go on throughout the night, and the celebrations can last for several days.

Tobaski
(Id-ul-Adha)

The festival of Tobaski, or Id-ul-Adha, is another important celebration for Muslims in West Africa. It marks the time when Allah tested the prophet Abraham by asking him to kill his own son. He only stopped Abraham at the last moment. Abraham sacrificed a sheep instead.

Today at Tobaski, there is a special feast. The head of the household slaughters a goat or a sheep, which is eaten at the meal. Sometimes it is cooked in a peanut sauce, or it is cooked with vegetables such as eggplant or cassava.

▲ Snacks of small fish pies, doughnuts, and popcorn are prepared for visitors on special occasions in Gambia.

This man has just bought a goat at a market in Gambia, for the feast of Tobaski.

Chicken *yassa* is a favorite dish in Gambia.

Id-ul-Fitr in Gambia

In Gambia, Muslim people celebrate Id-ul-Fitr by eating a special lunch dish, called *nyankantango*, which means "ten types of food." The dish includes smoked fish, rice, locust beans, peanuts, and palm kernel oil. Another favorite is chicken *yassa*, which is chicken in lemon juice. There is a recipe for chicken *yassa* on the opposite page. People also enjoy a sweet drink, called *ngalakh*, which is made with millet, peanuts, and fruit.

Chicken Yassa

EQUIPMENT
Lemon squeezer
Chopping knife
Chopping board
Large dish
Frying pan
Strainer

INGREDIENTS

4 chicken pieces
Juice of 2 lemons
1 onion, chopped

Salt and pepper
3 tablespoons of cooking oil
Cup of water

Pour the lemon juice over the chicken pieces. Then spread on the chopped onion and add the oil. Put this chicken mixture in the refrigerator.

Leave the chicken in the refrigerator for at least two hours. Then take the chicken out of the sauce and ask an adult to brown it under a hot broiler.

Drain the onions in a strainer and reserve the sauce. Fry the onions until they are soft. Add the sauce and cook for 5 minutes.

Add the chicken pieces and a cup of water. Add a little salt and cover and simmer for 45 minutes. Add more water if necessary.

Always be careful with knives and hot pans. Ask an adult to help you.

Easter in Sierra Leone

Many people in West Africa, especially in the south, are Christians. Their religion, Christianity, was brought to West Africa by Europeans.

Easter is a Christian festival, which celebrates the time when Jesus came back to life after dying on the cross. In some countries, such as Nigeria, Ghana, and Sierra Leone, Easter is a public holiday. In Freetown, the capital city of Sierra Leone, Easter is a very popular celebration. Families gather to spend time together.

People leaving church on Easter Day in Ghana

Good Friday

After church on Good Friday, children make life-sized rag dolls from recycled materials. The doll represents Judas, who betrayed Jesus. Later, the doll is destroyed to show that Judas has been punished.

Many people do not eat meat on Good Friday, so dishes usually contain fish instead. The main meal of the day is called *olele*. This is a dish made with black-eyed beans, fish, chilies, and onions, which is eaten with sweet potatoes and plantains. Another popular dish is fish pepper soup, made with hot chilies. A recipe is on page 20.

This spicy fish pepper soup is often eaten on Good Friday.

Fish Pepper Soup

EQUIPMENT
Chopping board
Chopping knife
Large saucepan
Cup

INGREDIENTS

1 lb. white, boneless fish, cut into cubes

4 cups of water

2 tomatoes

1 onion, peeled

4 sprigs of parsley

2 chilies, chopped

2 teaspoons of salt

1 teaspoon of dried thyme

Ask an adult to chop the chilies for you. The juice will sting if you get it in your eyes or in any cuts.

Wash the fish and place it in the saucepan with the water.

Finely chop the tomatoes, onions, and parsley, and add them to the fish with the chopped chilies.

Add the salt and thyme and stir.

Bring the soup to a boil, cover, and simmer for 20 minutes.

Always be careful with hot pans and knives. Ask an adult to help you.

Easter Monday

Easter Monday is fun in Sierra Leone. It's "picnic day," when many people pack picnic baskets, along with a kite, and go to the beach. They fill the basket with special food, which is too expensive to have every day. They might have chicken or crab, snapper, or barracuda. These fish can be found in the seas around Freetown and are special favorites.

On the beach, people fly kites, enjoy their picnics, or have barbecues. Young people wander up and down the beach selling peanuts and fruits such as mangoes and pineapples.

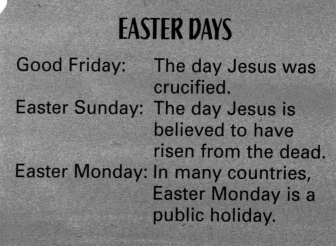

EASTER DAYS

Good Friday: The day Jesus was crucified.

Easter Sunday: The day Jesus is believed to have risen from the dead.

Easter Monday: In many countries, Easter Monday is a public holiday.

Children selling snacks to the tourists on the beach in Gambia

Naming Ceremonies

From Nigeria to Senegal, people celebrate the naming of a baby with a special ceremony. Usually, this takes place when the baby is about a week old. It is an occasion for people to eat the best food they can afford.

A baby's head is anointed with coconut in a naming ceremony in Gambia.

Friends, family, and important people in the village all gather together. Everyone whispers a special wish into the baby's ear. It might be "Have a long life" or "Be happy."

Special food

The Yoruba people, who live in southern Nigeria, eat special food to represent different wishes for the baby. They pass around bowls of different foods, and everyone has a small taste. They eat honey so that the baby will have a sweet life, palm oil so that the baby's life will be smooth and easy, and salt so that it will be interesting and full of savor.

FIFTH BIRTHDAYS

In some countries, such as Nigeria, people have a special celebration on a child's fifth birthday. That is because many children die from diseases before they are five. So if a child reaches this age, it is seen as a big achievement.

A basket of palm kernels (left) and oil made from them (right) in Sierra Leone

Feast!

In Muslim communities there is a feast after the baby has been named. People eat goat meat. But first the meat is offered to the oldest man in the community, to show respect. Pounded yam with okra soup, rice with pepper, or fried plantains are all popular dishes at naming ceremonies. There is a recipe for fried plantains on the opposite page.

▲ Plantains being grilled over hot charcoal in Ghana

WEIGHT IN GOLD

In Gambia, a baby's head is sometimes shaved. The hair is weighed, and the equivalent value in gold is given to the poor.

This baby belongs to the ▶ Wodaabe people, in Niger.

Fried Plantain

INGREDIENTS

4 large plantains or bananas

4 Tablespoons brown sugar

1 teaspoon of cinnamon

4 Tablespoons butter or margarine

EQUIPMENT

Frying pan   Wooden spoon

Chopping board   Spatula

Knife

1 Peel the plantains or bananas and cut them in half lengthwise.

2 Melt the butter in the frying pan. Add the sugar and half the cinnamon. Cook until the sugar has melted, stirring constantly.

3 Add the plantains or bananas, spoon the sugar mixture over them, and fry for about a minute.

4 Serve the plantains or bananas on a plate, with the rest of the cinnamon sprinkled on top.

Be careful when frying. Ask an adult to help you.

Yam Festivals

Yams are such an essential food that anyone who is good at growing them is thought to be a very important person. In Nigeria, Ghana, and Sierra Leone, yam festivals are held in August, when the new yams are ready to be harvested. The period before the harvest is called the "hungry months." People living in towns try to return to their home villages to celebrate the yam festival.

The seeds of yams are planted in mounds so that they can grow properly. The mounds keep the seeds cool and rain runs off.

Harvest

On the day of the yam festival, the women of each village get up very early and go to the fields to harvest the yams. They dig them out of the ground, using hoes, and dust off the earth. Then, they hold a short ceremony in the fields.

This Nigerian woman is deep-frying yams. Deep-fried yams are called *dunduns*.

The ceremony

Traditionally, people in Africa believe that their ancestors are very important. So when they have a successful harvest of yams, they thank their ancestors at the yam festival. The new yams are placed on special stools, and the ancestors are thanked with a short chant and with singing.

After the ceremony, a child is chosen to carry the new yams home. Then everyone rushes home to cook the new yams, along with other favorite dishes, such as fruit salads. There is a recipe for fruit salad on the opposite page. People sing traditional songs of thanks and visit their friends. There is dancing and feasting late into the night.

YAM FESTIVAL ABROAD

Many Nigerians living in other countries like to celebrate the yam festival by having a special meal for friends. If they can find some yams, they may use them to make the pounded-yam dish *fufu*.

Fruit salads like this are eaten at the yam festival.

Fruit Salad

INGREDIENTS

4 ripe mangoes

4 bananas

1 large tomato

1/2 pineapple, cut into cubes

Juice from 1 lime

1 cup of water

1 cup of sugar

1 cup of shredded coconut

EQUIPMENT

Chopping knife

Chopping board

Large bowl

Pitcher

Wooden spoon

1

Wash and peel the mangoes and chop the flesh into bite-sized pieces. Peel and slice the bananas.

2

Cut the tomato in half, remove the seeds, and cut it into cubes. Mix the tomato and all the fruit together in a large bowl.

3

In a pitcher, mix the lime juice with the water and sugar to make a dressing. Stir well.

4

Pour the dressing over the fruit, cover the bowl and refrigerate for at least one hour. Sprinkle the shredded coconut on the top just before serving.

Always be careful with knives. Ask an adult to help.

Glossary

Ancestors Family members who died a long time ago.

Calabashes The dried and hollowed-out shells of gourds (a type of fruit), which are used as containers.

Crucified Put to death on a cross, as a punishment.

Fast To go without food for a period of time, often for religious reasons.

Grain The small, hard seed from various types of grasses, which people can cook and eat.

Harvest The collecting of grain, fruit, and vegetables when they are ripe and ready to eat.

Nomads People who move from place to place to find food and water supplies.

Okra A type of vegetable with long, green pods.

Plantain A tropical fruit like a banana, but not so sweet.

Plantations Very large farms.

Preserve To treat food in a way that allows it to be kept for a long time before it spoils.

Protein The essential part of a diet that helps us to grow.

Rain forests Thick forests that grow in the tropical areas of the world, where the climate is hot and very wet.

Winnowing Separating grain from the rest of the plant by tossing it into the air. The wind blows away the stalks and the heavier grain falls into the basket.

Author acknowledgments
The author would like to thank the following for their advice, support, and information: Lucy Faemata Davies, Ivan Scott, Fenella White, Morounke Williams, Sam Woodhouse, and the Marlborough Brandt Group.
Photograph and artwork acknowledgments
The publishers would like to thank the following for contributing to the pictures in this book:
Axiom *title page*/James H. Morris, 21/Steve J. Benbow, 22/James Morris; Antony Blake *contents page*, 27; Chapel Studios/Zul Mukhida 16, 19, 28; Robert Estall 24 (bottom)/Carol Beckwith; Eye Ubiquitous 5 (centre left)/Tim Durham, 8/Tim Durham; Hutchison 12, 18/Timothy Beddow; Impact 11/Giles Morley; Christine Osborne 14, 23; Panos *cover*/Ron Giling, 5(top left)/Betty Press, 5(bottom left)/Liba Taylor, 5(centre right)/Jeremy Hartley, 5(bottom right)/Ron Giling, 7/Betty Press, 9(top)/Liba Taylor, 9(bottom)/Jeremy Hartley, 10/Marcus Rose, 13/Marcus Rose, 26/Bruce Paton; Peter Sanders 6; Trip 24(bottom)/B. Seed; Wayland Picture Library 5 (top right), 15/James Morris.
Fruit and vegetable artwork is by Tina Barber. Map artwork on page 4 is by Hardlines.
Step-by-step recipe artwork is by Judy Stevens.

Books to Read

Chambers, Catherine. *Easter* (World of Holidays). Austin, TX: Raintree Steck-Vaughn, 1998.

Diagram Group. *Peoples of West Africa*. New York: Facts on File, 1997.

Kerven, Rosalind. *Id-ul-Fitr* (World of Holidays). Austin, TX: Raintree Steck-Vaughn, 1997.

Knight, Khadijah. *Islamic Festivals* (Celebrate). New York: Heinemann Library, 1997.

Penney, Sue. *Islam* (Discovering Religions). Austin, TX: Raintree Steck-Vaughn, 1996.

Tames, Richard and Tames, Sheila. *Muslim* (Beliefs and Cultures). Danbury, CT: Children's Press, 1997.

Tenquist, Alisdair. *Nigeria* (Economically Developing Countries). Austin, TX: Raintree Steck-Vaughn, 1996.

Thompson, Jan. *Christian Festivals* (Celebrate). New York: Heinemann Library, 1997.

Index

Page numbers in **bold** mean there is a photograph on the page.

barbecues 21

camels **6**
Cameroon 12
cassava 5, **5**, 8, **8**, 15
cattle 5, 9
chickens 9, 16, 21
Christians 18–19
climate 6
corn 5, 7

dishes
  chicken *yassa* 16, **16**, 17
  deep-fried yams
    (*dunduns*) **27**
  fish pepper soup 19, **19**,
    20
  fried plantains 24, **24**, 25
  fruit salad 28, **28**, 29
  fufu 8, 28
  Ngalakh 16
  nyankantango 16
  okra soup 24
  olele 19

Easter 18, 21

fasting 12
festivals 8, 10, **10**
fish 5, **5**, 10, 15, **15**, 16,
  19, 21
fruit 5, **5**, 16, 21, 28

Gambia 11, 15, **15**, 16,
  21, 22, 24
Ghana 8, 9, 18, 24, 26
goats 5, **5**, 9, **9**, 15, **15**, 24
Good Friday 19
Guinea 8

Id-ul-Fitr 13–14, 16
Islam 11

Mali 7
Mauritania 6
millet 5, 7, **7**, 16
Muslims 11, **11**, 12, 13,
  15, 16, 24

naming ceremonies 22–24

Niger 24
Nigeria 10, 11, 13, 14, 18,
  22, 23, 26, 27, 28

palm kernel oil 16, 23, **23**
peanuts **5**, 8, **9**, 16, 21
plantains 19, 24, **24**

Ramadan 12–13
recipes
  chicken *yassa* 17
  fish pepper soup 20
  fried plantains 25
  fruit salad 29
rice 7, 16, 24

Senegal 9, 11, 22
Sierra Leone 8, 18–19,
  21, 23, 26

Tobaski (Id-ul-Adha) 15, **15**

yams 5, 8, 24, 26–28,
  27, **27**